MY OCEAN LINER
Across the North Atlantic on the Great Ship Normandie

A Story by PETER MANDEL
Illustrated by BETSEY MacDONALD

INTRODUCTION BY JOHN MAXTONE-GRAHAM

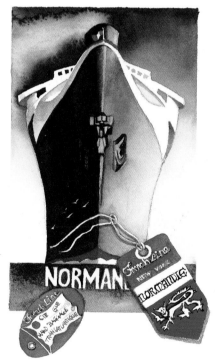

Stemmer House

PUBLISHERS
OWINGS MILLS, MARYLAND

Inquiries should be directed to
Stemmer House Publishers, Inc.
2627 Caves Road
Owings Mills, Maryland 21117-2919

A Barbara Holdridge book
First Edition
Printed in Hong Kong

Acknowledgments: Special thanks to John Maxtone-Graham, who steered the author, illustrator and publisher with a firm hand to the home port of Exactitude in
matters nautical. Any errors that may remain must be attributed solely to our own
faulty reckoning. We are indebted also to the John Maxtone-Graham Collection
for permission to reproduce the photograph of the *Normandie* on page 9.

Library of Congress Cataloging-in-Publication Data

Mandel, Peter, 1957–
    My ocean liner : across the North Atlantic on the great ship Normandie / a story by
  Peter Mandel; illustrated by Betsey MacDonald.
        p. cm.
    "A Barbara Holdridge book."
    Summary: In 1939, nine-year-old Paul goes on a memorable five-day voyage from New
  York to France on the luxurious ocean liner Normandie, the biggest ship in the world.
    ISBN 0-88045-149-1 (hardbound)
    [1. Normandie (Steamship)—Fiction. 2. Ocean liners—Fiction. 3. Ocean
  travel—Fiction.] I. MacDonald, Betsey ill. II. Title.

PZ7.M31223 My 2000
[Fic]—dc21
                                                                    00-055644

CONTENTS

Author's Dedication
In memory of my father,
Paul William Mandel,
who taught me
to love ships

INTRODUCTION

For those of us who cherish ocean liners, *Normandie* remains forever a paradigm of elegance, chic and stylishness, boasting the most compelling maritime design scheme ever conceived. She was the first 1,000-foot passenger vessel and she was also the world's fastest. Additionally, she retains a potent mystique that, more than half a century after her unkind demise of 1942, has never been equaled. *Normandie* remains one of an historic kind, the quintessential North Atlantic liner.

The French Line was famous for cossetting its passengers and, aboard that 1935 flagship, the Line's legendary concern was, if anything, amplified. First-class clients patronizing *Normandie*'s elevator were conducted into the conveyance by a scarlet-jacketed *mousse* (bellboy), who served as a personal guide to the passenger's destination. Thanks to the zeal of ferocious *chef de cuisine* Gaston Maigran, no higher gastronomic standard existed anywhere. French Line pursers—called *commissaires* in French—were renowned for their tact, diplomacy, dedication and flawless social instincts. Ring Lardner penned a rhyme about *Normandie*'s chief purser, when he served aboard a previous vessel: "Here's to Villar, the *France*'s great purser / But oh how much more than a purser you were sir!"

At least *My Ocean Liner*'s young protagonist never shared the distress of another small boy who, embarking on *Normandie*, burst into tears, demanding to know where the ship was. Though children are bound to be entranced by this evocation in narrative and fine illustrations of *Normandie* passage, the volume will also find shelf space in the libraries of many adults—a children's book that transcends juvenilia by appealing to grown bibliophiles as well.

The Hudson is sparkling, the flags are flying, the whistle is blowing and the tugs are ready: Grab your luggage and race aboard *Normandie* for the crossing of your life!

New York City, 2000   JOHN MAXTONE-GRAHAM

Chapter One

THE GANGWAY: NEW YORK

Paul! Wake up! Look out the window!" It was my dad getting me up early to see the huge *Normandie*—our own ocean liner—sliding into its Hudson River dock. Dad and I hung out the window, wide awake, excited and waiting for the whistle to blow.

It was April, and the year was 1939. I was nine years old. My mom and dad and I would be leaving our apartment on Manhattan's West Side to visit France and England. In those  days, nobody traveled to Europe by airplane. People sailed across the Atlantic in huge ships called ocean liners. I couldn't stop thinking about it.

"The trip will take five days," my mom told me, as she was stuffing an extra sweater and some socks into my suitcase. "Sailing on the *Normandie* will be a real adventure."

"She's the biggest ship in the world," said my

dad, who had come to tuck me in. "As big as an office building or a hotel–but this hotel can float!"

When the lights were out, I thought about what would happen the next morning. I had been to Pier 88, where we would go aboard, so I knew what that looked like. But it was hard to imagine being up close to a ship as big as a building or a hotel. In my dream that night, I climbed steps and more steps, trying to climb high enough to get on board.

In our taxi the next day, my dad put his hand on my shoulder. Looming behind the piers along the Hudson River, I saw a huge white-and-black shape.

When three red smokestacks came into view, I knew we were looking at a French liner–*my* ocean liner–the *Normandie.*

Going aboard was not like my dream at all. There were no stairs to climb; only an enclosed ramp called a gangway. Through an opening, we could look down at waves sloshing between the metal hull of the ship and the dock. I ran the last few yards of the gangway until I was safely aboard.

"Let's get the luggage stowed, and then we're going right up on deck," said my dad. "I don't want Paul to miss the tugboats."

Just then we saw young men wearing uniforms with silver buttons walking quickly past us in the hall way. One of them was banging on a Chinese gong. "Visitors will please leave the ship," another of them kept crying out. "All ashore that's going ashore!"

Chapter Two

THE DEAUVILLE SUITE: UNDERWAY

My dad held me right against the deck railing, so I could lean over a little and look down. Below I saw three small boats with fat smokestacks and round rubber bumpers. "Watch them work," Dad said. "And listen."

Suddenly, all the noise of the pier was drowned out by a tremendous blast on the ship's whistle: *"Booooooooooooommmmmmph!"* I clapped my hands over my ears, and so did my mom.

The engines of the tugboats came to life. I saw water churning, and as the tugs moved close to guide her, the *Normandie* made a magical slide backward into the Hudson River. My mom pointed out a traffic light on the end of the pier that let ships' masters know the river was clear of traffic.

Soon the big ship was out in the Hudson River and making a wide turn. People were crowding the

railing, waving to friends on the pier. My parents and I waved too.

As the *Normandie* began its trip down the Hudson, my mom and dad and I went below deck to relax in our cabin and take a good look around. It was really a suite of rooms, called the Deauville Suite. It seemed large and comfortable, with wood paneling, upholstered chairs, cream-colored blankets with the French Line logo, a piano and windows through which we could look out on New York harbor. I could see a ferry chugging back from Staten Island, and the awesome Statue of Liberty holding up her torch.

Right near the door, I noticed a panel with two small buzzers—one red and one green.  My mom had noticed them, too. "Push one," she suggested. "Let's see what happens."

Because the *Normandie* had red smokestacks, I picked the red buzzer and pushed. Soon there was a knock on our door.

Chapter Three

THE DINING ROOM: AT SEA

C abin steward," said a voice with a French accent, and in popped a young man wearing a trim uniform jacket and cap. "I am Pascal," he announced. "Would you like some *thé* or *chocolat chaud*? Perhaps a small snack?"

"Thank you very much for asking," I replied, "but I guess I was more curious than hungry."

From talking to Pascal, I found out that the green buzzer called a stewardess, Nicole, who could draw a bath for you, sew up a hole in your shirt or give you a copy of the ship's daily newspaper, *L'Atlantique*.

I began to feel the *Normandie* rise and sink with the waves, and Pascal showed me how to hold onto the railing outside our cabin. After a while, my mom warned me it was nearly dinner time. "I need to ask

Pascal one more question," I said. "Is that an officer's hat you have on?"

"No, no," answered Pascal. "It is only a steward's cap. But would you like to try it?"

The bill of the cap came down low over my eyes. But for a second, I felt like a real crew member on the *Normandie.*

The dining room was not like any restaurant I had ever seen. It was much longer, with mirrors everywhere, a great bronze statue at the entrance and tall columns of lights between the tables. This first night no one was dressed up; but the other nights, my mom said, the ladies would wear gowns and the men black jackets and pants, with black or white bow ties.

Our waiter brought menus and a basket of rolls that were called *petit pain,* with crusts so brittle that they just about exploded when I broke them open to butter them. We watched him weave in and out

19

among all the other waiters carrying trays with soup bowls filled to the brim. Even though the ship was swaying, no one spilled a drop.

While I was taking my first bite of steak *au poivre* (it was peppery, but very good), the ship began to roll even more, and plates and cups began sliding. But because each table had *cabarets*—hinged, raised edges on all sides, like little fences—nothing was falling into our laps or onto the floor!

Chapter four

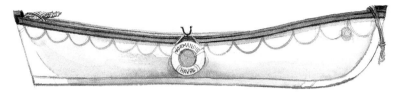

THE SUN DECK: AT SEA

Our first night at sea, the *Normandie* rose and dipped and rolled dangerously from side to side. At first, I gripped the side of my bed, thinking I might tumble out. Before long, I realized that either my mom or dad had tucked my blankets in tightly, and I relaxed enough to fall asleep.

My mom woke me up early, and I didn't feel well. "I think you're a little bit seasick," she said, stroking my hair. "It happens to nearly everyone their first time on board ship."

"I don't feel too chipper myself," said my dad. "I'm afraid there's only one cure for us, and that's salt air. Let's head out to the Sun Deck."

My dad and I went outside, and we were almost knocked off our feet by the wind. I started counting lifeboats, until I convinced myself there were enough for everyone, and then I looked beyond them at an ocean of blue-green waves with caps of white foam. I breathed in the crisp salt air for what seemed a long while. My dad was right. I didn't feel sick anymore.

"I think you've got your sea legs, Paul," said my dad. I would have felt proud, but I saw that the other passengers were even more comfortable with life on an ocean liner. There were loud games of ping-pong being played. And there was another game I didn't recognize: people were using wooden sticks to push disks up and down the deck.

A boy in white flannel pants invited me to play, and soon I was sliding disks with everyone else and laughing when my disk knocked someone else's away and gave me the highest score. People were clapping and I heard someone call out, *"Magnifique, magnifique!"*

After the game was over, my dad told me that the game I'd been playing was called shuffleboard. As we walked away, I saw that the other boy was tugging hard on the handle of a very small door on deck. It wasn't a door for passengers. I could see that. But it opened, and he disappeared.

Chapter Five

THE BRIDGE: AT SEA

In a hallway, my dad and I suddenly collided with a stewardess who was in a big hurry. When she stopped to apologize, we realized it was *our* stewardess, Nicole.

"I am looking for someone in another part of the ship," she told us. "Perhaps Paul would like to come along?" Before I could say yes, Nicole had taken me by the hand. I felt a tug, and soon she was whisking me through carpeted corridors and down staircases.

Nicole rapped on a metal doorway and a sailor with a white cap and red pompom talked to her in low tones and then let us in. I was excited to see a long, curving room, with windows along one wall and instruments of all kinds, covered in brass. There were no passengers, only ship's officers in navy-blue uniforms, gold braid decorating their caps and sleeves.

"I heard the announcement," Nicole said to one of the officers. He nodded his head. "And still no one has seen Robert anywhere aboard ship?"

"I am afraid that is correct," said the officer, removing his cap and wiping his forehead with one sleeve. Then he turned to me.

"I am Quartermaster Pierre Duval," he said. "Welcome aboard our ship." My mouth opened and closed, but nothing came out.

"A-are you really one of the officers in command?" I asked, after a second or two. "And is this the bridge where you steer the *Normandie*?"

"The answer is yes to both questions," said Quartermaster Duval. "Do you have any others you would like to ask?"

When I told him I had been counting lifeboats,

he threw back his head and laughed. "We have more than enough lifeboats for all 1,800 passengers, the crew and for stowaways, too! This is not the *Titanic*, but the *Normandie!* Tell me, would you like to try putting your hands on the ship's wheel, while I take the helm?"

My eyes opened wide, and I nodded quickly, without speaking. Although I didn't really know what the Quartermaster meant, just being on the bridge was better than anything I had ever imagined before we'd left New York!

Taking the helm meant actually *steering the ship*, I discovered. When I mounted a platform and felt my hands on the wooden, spoked wheel, I imagined how it would feel if I were really guiding that huge ship, but I knew it was up to my great new friend, the Quartermaster, to make sure the *Normandie* stayed on course.

Chapter Six

THE ENGINE ROOM: AT SEA

Quartermaster Duval saw that I was eyeing one of the shiny brass instruments with a puzzled expression. "This important instrument is the throttle. It is the engine room telegraph, which sends the order to make the *Normandie* go fast or slow."

I saw that it was set at "Full Speed Ahead," and the Quartermaster explained that it would stay that way for most of the voyage.

Now he introduced me to an even higher ranking officer, Staff Captain Jean Moulin. "Buzz me at once," he said to a sailor, "if Robert is found."

Then he asked us to follow him. With Nicole taking me by the hand, the three of us squeezed into the tiniest elevator I had ever been in.

When the door slid open, I smelled oil. I knew from the noise and heat that we were entering the Engine Room. Some men in overalls looked up from cleaning a metal part that was coated with grease. They seemed surprised to see an officer. All of them

stood at attention, trying to wipe their hands on their shirts.

"When I give a command up on the bridge," he explained, "it's relayed down here. The engine burns more oil, the propeller turns faster, and more smoke pours out of—what?"

"The smokestacks!" I guessed. He smiled.

Riding the elevator back up, I suddenly remembered the boy I'd played shuffleboard with.

"That Robert, the one you're looking for," I said to Nicole and the officer. "Is he around my age?"

"Indeed!" answered the Staff Captain, lifting one bushy eyebrow so high it brushed the bill of his cap.

"And does he have blonde hair and white pants?"

"*Oui, oui!* Yes!" said Nicole. Now it was my turn to take Nicole by the hand. And I led her right to the small hatch on deck.

"It is too low for me," she said. "Here is a flashlight. Can you reach in and see if Robert is there?"

I got down and poked next to some dusty steam pipes. I felt one life jacket; then a whole stack. And then a small voice said, "Ouch!" and I jumped up and banged my head. I had grabbed a foot!

Chapter Seven

THE SUN DECK: RESCUE AT SEA

Robert's clothes were snagged on something in the small, dark passageway. "I'm stuck," he moaned, and I could tell that he was really scared.

"Don't worry, we'll get you out of there," I said,

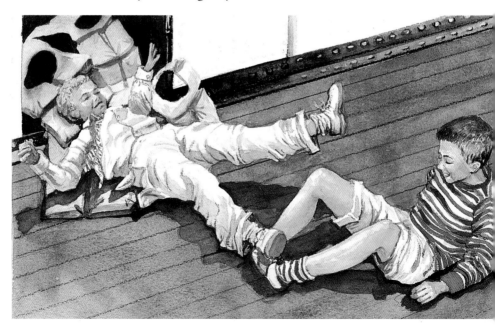

though I didn't have the slightest idea how. But then I had a thought.

I could hear that Pascal was outside now. I yelled for him to grab Nicole's arm and for her to take hold of mine. When I had my other hand around Robert's wrist, we all pulled and pulled just as hard as we could. We could feel the ship tipping one way and then the other. But we kept on tugging.

All of a sudden, there was a *ripping* sound—and all four of us fell back out on deck, along with a bunch of life jackets.

When Nicole picked Robert up and gave him a hug, we could see he was okay. But his white pants were not!

Chapter Eight

THE STORM: AT SEA

Rain had started to come down in big, fat drops. Before we knew what had happened, a North Atlantic storm was tossing the huge *Normandie* back and forth like a sailboat. Waves had grown into round green mountains and spray soaked everyone on deck.

A crew member rushed past. "It would be safer below deck!" he shouted, just as the ship lurched to one side and Nicole, Robert and I slipped on the wet planking. When a gigantic burst of spray surged high over the railing, I felt myself sliding *toward* it, since the boat was on a steep slant.

Pascal grabbed my belt and gripped tightly, as the boat rolled the other way and water poured overboard. The next thing I knew, Robert and I were in my cabin, wrapped in warm blankets.

"Thank goodness for Pascal," said my mom, who was toweling my hair. "You boys nearly went for a swim!"

"No, no," said Pascal. "Thank goodness for *Paul*. He is the real hero of the day. If it weren't for Paul, Robert here would still be lost!"

"So what made you go into that crawl space anyway, Robert?" I asked. "What were you looking for?"

"Gosh, Paul. Do you remember how you were counting lifeboats? I just thought I would do that with the lifejackets I saw the sailors put in there. I thought I'd count them, just like you. I didn't mean to get stuck in there and worry everyone—and ruin my good pants!"

After that, even though the gale was getting worse, someone took my picture for the ship's newspaper—and my dad told me he was *extremely* proud.

Chapter Nine

THE QUEEN MARY: AT SEA

The storm lasted past midnight. But the next day, when passengers were allowed out on deck, we saw that the ocean had become as blue and smooth as a sheet of glass.

Just then, the ship's whistle let out a blast.

"*Baaaaaaaaaaaaaaaaammmmmmmmmmmph!*"

An even deeper horn answered back.

"*Booooooooooooooooooommmmmmmmmmmmph!*"

"Look, Paul," shouted my dad. "Look what's passing us going from east to west!"

I saw another ocean liner, with three orange smokestacks, steaming towards us.

"You are lucky to see the *Queen Mary*," said a familiar voice. "I think the storm has blown her a little off course."

I turned to see Pascal and Nicole, who had come to tell us that they would be very happy to help us with our packing,

since we would be docking tomorrow at Le Havre. They could manage everything for us this evening. Tomorrow they would be busy cleaning all of the suites and cabins on our deck.

"And you must watch for the lights of the harbor tonight," said Nicole. "They are most beautiful."

"And very romantic," added Pascal, with a wink.

When they had walked some distance away, I saw that they were holding hands.

Chapter Ten

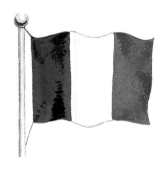

THE GANGWAY: LE HAVRE

After sunset, my family and I saw something we hadn't seen for a week—lights along the horizon. The *Normandie* was approaching Le Havre, where we would board a train for Paris.

On the gangway the next day, I looked up at the ship for the last time. I found the bridge, hoping that Quartermaster Duval was still there. But he must be off-duty by now, I thought. Robert must be packing his white flannel pants, neatly repaired by Nicole. And Pascal and Nicole must be too busy cleaning cabins to say goodbye. I turned away. My dad said to hurry or we would miss the train.

Suddenly, I heard some shouting in French. A man on the Boat Deck had tossed something overboard. It was folded like a paper airplane, and it fluttered in the wind.

37

It was a letter, and this is what it said:

Dear Paul,

We hope your trip on the Normandie *was an adventure you will not forget. To remind you of your voyage when you are in Paris, you and your parents must come to our wedding at St. Severin Church on the Left Bank at 3 o'clock one week from today!*

Love,

Nicole et Pascal

Even though my sea legs hadn't yet become land legs, I hurried just as my dad had told me to, waving the white paper as I ran.

EPILOGUE

Years and years have passed since my voyage on the *Normandie*, now long gone. In 1942, during the Second World War, while she was being outfitted at Pier 88 in New York to carry troops, the great ship caught fire and capsized, never to sail again.

But Pascal, Nicole and I are old, old friends, even though they live in a suburb of Paris, France and I in a Manhattan apartment with a view of today's cruise ships making their way up and down the Hudson River.

I am happy to say that Pascal and Nicole named the youngest of their four children Paul. And I like to suppose that it was in honor of me and of the exciting time when we met.

By the way, I have great plans for young Paul. Now that he is old enough, I plan to take him on an ocean crossing of his own. But this one will take only eight hours instead of five whole days.

That's right. You guessed it. We will cross the Atlantic from Paris by jet.

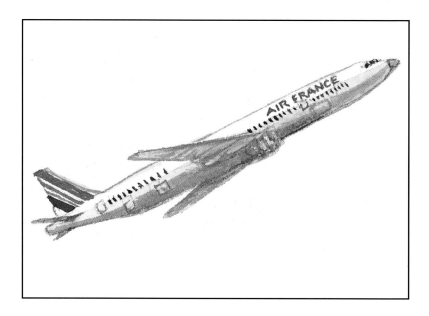

Though I am looking forward to our flight, I yearn to sail again, even after flying one of those great jet planes of the air. So for our return from New

York, I have booked us tickets on the *Queen Elizabeth 2*—an ocean liner that is so much like the *Normandie* that I can hardly wait.

Watch for us pulling out if you are down by the pier. And listen for our whistle. It will be *l o u d* and *l o n g*.

41

GLOSSARY

BOW (pronounced like "now")   Front of a ship

BRIDGE   A ship's control room that is normally high up and near the front of the vessel. The BRIDGE has many windows and is where the captain or officer on duty navigates, using maps and instruments.

GALE   A big storm at sea, with high winds

GALLEY   The kitchen area of a ship, where meals are prepared

GANGWAY   A walkway that bridges the gap between ship and pier, allowing passengers and crew to board and disembark

GETTING YOUR LAND LEGS   Once you've been on board ship for some time, it's sometimes hard to balance when you arrive in port, until you "GET YOUR LAND LEGS back."

GETTING YOUR SEA LEGS   Getting used to the rolling motion of the ship, so that you can walk normally, just as if you were on land

HELM   Taking the HELM of a ship means taking control: making decisions on steering, speed, etc.

HORIZON   The distant line where sea or land seems to be meeting the sky.

HULL   The body or "frame" of a ship

INTERNATIONAL FLAG CODE   A system of using 36 flags and pennants, representing letters and numerals, to send messages. The word "Glossary," page 42, is spelled out in INTERNATIONAL FLAG CODE.

KNOT   A measurement of speed used by ships at sea. A KNOT equals one NAUTICAL MILE per hour.

LEEWARD   The LEEWARD side of a ship is the side furthest away from wind direction.

LIFEBOATS   Small boats kept on board ship in case an emergency forces passengers and crew to escape by BOARDING THE LIFEBOATS. Ships are required to have LIFEBOAT DRILLS, to acquaint passengers with lifejackets and lifeboat stations.

LIFEJACKETS   Worn in an emergency, LIFEJACKETS fit over the head and shoulders. Each one is foam-filled, has a bell and a light, and keeps the wearer afloat while he or she is waiting to be rescued.

OFF COURSE   The ship is heading in the wrong direction.

ON COURSE   The ship is going in the right direction.

PORT SIDE   The left side of a ship, looking forward

PORTHOLE   A watertight window used on ships

SEA SALT   Someone who has lived and worked at or near the sea for many years, loves it and has soaked up the seafaring way of life

SHUFFLEBOARD   A shipboard game played on the deck, using long sticks with curved fronts to slide wooden disks toward numbered squares. When the disk lands in a square, the player gets the number of points indicated, and the one with the most points wins.

STARBOARD   The right side of a ship, looking forward

STOW   To put something away neatly and securely aboard ship

STOWAWAY   Someone who sneaks on board a ship and hides, in order to get a free trip

VESSEL   A ship or boat

VOYAGE   A trip taken by sea

WAKE   The choppy water behind a moving ship, caused by the spinning propellers and the hull passing through the water

WINDWARD   The WINDWARD side of a ship is the side closest to the direction from which the wind is blowing.

French words, phrases and names in *My Ocean Liner*

AU REVOIR   Goodbye, or "Till we meet again"

BONJOUR   Hello

44

GLOSSARY

CABARETS   The French word for the hinged table-edges that keep plates, silver and glasses from sliding off the dining table when the ship is rolling

CHOCOLAT CHAUD   Hot chocolate

L'ATLANTIQUE   The Atlantic Ocean

LEFT BANK   The famous "*Rive Gauche*," on the left bank of the River Seine. This Paris neighborhood is the traditional home of many artists and writers.

MAGNIFIQUE   Magnificent

NON   No

OUI   Yes

PETIT PAIN   Bread rolls

ST. SEVERIN CHURCH   A large, historic and very beautiful church in Paris, France

S'IL VOUS PLAÎT   Please

STEAK AU POIVRE   Steak sautéed with black pepper and finished with a rich sauce

THÉ   Tea

DESIGNED BY BARBARA HOLDRIDGE
COMPOSED IN GARAMOND TEXT
WITH BONGO BLACK DISPLAY AND
BODONI MT ULTRA BOLD INITIALS
PREPRESS PRODUCTION BY THE
CLARINDA COMPANY, CLARINDA,
IOWA
PRINTED ON 86-POUND ACID-FREE
MATTE PAPER AND CASEBOUND BY
REGENT PUBLISHING SERVICES, HONG KONG